Layers of Learning

Year One • Unit Fifteen

First North Americans
North America
Salts
Creative Kids

HooDoo Publishing
United States of America
©2014 Layers of Learning
Copies of maps or activities may be made for a particular family or classroom.
ISBN 978-1495231049

If you wish to reproduce or print excerpts of this publication, please contact us at contact@layers-of-learning.com for permission. Thank you for respecting copyright laws.

Units At A Glance: Topics For All Four Years of the Layers of Learning Program

1	History	Geography	Science	The Arts
1	Mesopotamia	Maps & Globes	Planets	Cave Paintings
2	Egypt	Map Keys	Stars	Egyptian Art
3	Europe	Global Grids	Earth & Moon	Crafts
4	Ancient Greece	Wonders	Satellites	Greek Art
5	Babylon	Mapping People	Humans in Space	Poetry
6	The Levant	Physical Earth	Laws of Motion	List Poems
7	Phoenicians	Oceans	Motion	Moral Stories
8	Assyrians	Deserts	Fluids	Rhythm
9	Persians	Arctic	Waves	Melody
10	Ancient China	Forests	Machines	Chinese Art
11	Early Japan	Mountains	States of Matter	Line & Shape
12	Arabia	Rivers & Lakes	Atoms	Color & Value
13	Ancient India	Grasslands	Elements	Texture & Form
14	Ancient Africa	Africa	Bonding	African Tales
15	First North Americans	North America	Salts	Creative Kids
16	Ancient South America	South America	Plants	South American Art
17	Celts	Europe	Flowering Plants	Jewelry
18	Roman Republic	Asia	Trees	Roman Art
19	Christianity	Australia & Oceania	Simple Plants	Instruments
20	Roman Empire	You Explore	Fungi	Composing Music

2	History	Geography	Science	The Arts
1	Byzantines	Turkey	Climate & Seasons	Byzantine Art
2	Barbarians	Ireland	Forecasting	Illumination
3	Islam	Arabian Peninsula	Clouds & Precipitation	Creative Kids
4	Vikings	Norway	Special Effects	Viking Art
5	Anglo Saxons	Britain	Wild Weather	King Arthur Tales
6	Charlemagne	France	Cells and DNA	Carolingian Art
7	Normans	Nigeria	Skeletons	Canterbury Tales
8	Feudal System	Germany	Muscles, Skin, & Cardiopulmonary	Gothic Art
9	Crusades	Balkans	Digestive & Senses	Religious Art
10	Burgundy, Venice, Spain	Switzerland	Nerves	Oil Paints
11	Wars of the Roses	Russia	Health	Minstrels & Plays
12	Eastern Europe	Hungary	Metals	Printmaking
13	African Kingdoms	Mali	Carbon Chem	Textiles
14	Asian Kingdoms	Southeast Asia	Non-metals	Vivid Language
15	Mongols	Caucasus	Gases	Fun With Poetry
16	Medieval China & Japan	China	Electricity	Asian Arts
17	Pacific Peoples	Micronesia	Circuits	Arts of the Islands
18	American Peoples	Canada	Technology	Indian Legends
19	The Renaissance	Italy	Magnetism	Renaissance Art I
20	Explorers	Caribbean Sea	Motors	Renaissance Art II

3	History	Geography	Science	The Arts
1	Age of Exploration	Argentina and Chile	Classification & Insects	Fairy Tales
2	The Ottoman Empire	Egypt and Libya	Reptiles & Amphibians	Poetry
3	Mogul Empire	Pakistan & Afghanistan	Fish	Mogul Arts
4	Reformation	Angola & Zambia	Birds	Reformation Art
5	Renaissance England	Tanzania & Kenya	Mammals & Primates	Shakespeare
6	Thirty Years' War	Spain	Sound	Baroque Music
7	The Dutch	Netherlands	Light & Optics	Baroque Art I
8	France	Indonesia	Bending Light	Baroque Art II
9	The Enlightenment	Korean Pen.	Color	Art Journaling
10	Russia & Prussia	Central Asia	History of Science	Watercolors
11	Conquistadors	Baltic States	Igneous Rocks	Creative Kids
12	Settlers	Peru & Bolivia	Sedimentary Rocks	Native American Art
13	13 Colonies	Central America	Metamorphic Rocks	Settler Sayings
14	Slave Trade	Brazil	Gems & Minerals	Colonial Art
15	The South Pacific	Australasia	Fossils	Principles of Art
16	The British in India	India	Chemical Reactions	Classical Music
17	Boston Tea Party	Japan	Reversible Reactions	Folk Music
18	Founding Fathers	Iran	Compounds & Solutions	Rococo
19	Declaring Independence	Samoa and Tonga	Oxidation & Reduction	Creative Crafts I
20	The American Revolution	South Africa	Acids & Bases	Creative Crafts II

4	History	Geography	Science	The Arts
1	American Government	USA	Heat & Temperature	Patriotic Music
2	Expanding Nation	Pacific States	Motors & Engines	Tall Tales
3	Industrial Revolution	U.S. Landscapes	Energy	Romantic Art I
4	Revolutions	Mountain West States	Energy Sources	Romantic Art II
5	Africa	U.S. Political Maps	Energy Conversion	Impressionism I
6	The West	Southwest States	Earth Structure	Impressionism II
7	Civil War	National Parks	Plate Tectonics	Post-Impressionism
8	World War I	Plains States	Earthquakes	Expressionism
9	Totalitarianism	U.S. Economics	Volcanoes	Abstract Art
10	Great Depression	Heartland States	Mountain Building	Kinds of Art
11	World War II	Symbols and Landmarks	Chemistry of Air & Water	War Art
12	Modern East Asia	The South States	Food Chemistry	Modern Art
13	India's Independence	People of America	Industry	Pop Art
14	Israel	Appalachian States	Chemistry of Farming	Modern Music
15	Cold War	U.S. Territories	Chemistry of Medicine	Free Verse
16	Vietnam War	Atlantic States	Food Chains	Photography
17	Latin America	New England States	Animal Groups	Latin American Art
18	Civil Rights	Home State Study	Instincts	Theater & Film
19	Technology	Home State Study II	Habitats	Architecture
20	Terrorism	America in Review	Conservation	Creative Kids

Unit 1-15 Printable Pack

This unit includes printables at the end. To make life easier for you we also created digital printable packs for each unit. To retrieve your printable pack for Unit 1-15, please visit

www.layers-of-learning.com/digital-printable-packs/

Put the printable pack in your shopping cart and use this coupon code:

0115UNIT1-15

Your printable pack will be free.

Layers of Learning Introduction

This is part of a series of units in the Layers of Learning homeschool curriculum, including the subjects of history, geography, science, and the arts. Children from 1st through 12th can participate in the same curriculum at the same time – family school style.

The units are intended to be used in order as the basis of a complete curriculum (once you add in a systematic math, reading, and writing program). You begin with Year 1 Unit 1 no matter what ages your children are. Spend about 2 weeks on each unit. You pick and choose the activities within the unit that appeal to you and read the books from the book list that are available to you or find others on the same topic from your library. We highly recommend that you use the timeline in every history section as the backbone. Then flesh out your learning with reading and activities that highlight the topics you think are the most important.

Alternatively, you can use the units as activity ideas to supplement another curriculum in any order you wish. You can still use them with all ages of children at the same time.

When you've finished with Year One, move on to Year Two, Year Three, and Year Four. Then begin again with Year One and work your way through the years again. Now your children will be older, reading more involved books, and writing more in depth. When you have completed the sequence for the second time, you start again on it for the third and final time. If your student began with Layers of Learning in 1st grade and stayed with it all the way through she would go through the four year rotation three times, firmly cementing the information in her mind in ever increasing depth. At each level you should expect increasing amounts of outside reading and writing. High schoolers in particular should be reading extensively, and if possible, participating in discussion groups.

☺ ☺ ☺ These icons will guide you in spotting activities and books that are appropriate for the age of child you are working with. But if you think an activity is too juvenile or too difficult for your kids, adjust accordingly. The icons are not there as rules, just guides.

☺ Grades 1-4
☺ Grades 5-8
☺ Grades 9-12

Within each unit we share:
- EXPLORATIONS, activities relating to the topic;
- EXPERIMENTS, usually associated with science topics;
- EXPEDITIONS, field trips;
- EXPLANATIONS, teacher helps or educational philosophies.

In the sidebars we also include Additional Layers, Famous Folks, Fabulous Facts, On the Web, and other extra related topics that can take you off on tangents, exploring the world and your interests with a bit more freedom. The curriculum will always be there to pull you back on track when you're ready.

You can learn more about how to use this curriculum at www.layers-of-learning.com/layers-of-learning-program/

First North Americans – North America – Salts – Creative Kids

Unit Fifteen
First North Americans – North America – Salts – Creative Kids

I am a great believer in luck, and I find the harder I work the more I have of it.
-Thomas Jefferson

	Library List:
History	Search for: ancient Americans, early Americans, Bering Strait, Adena, Hopewell, Olmecs, Maya
	☺ Mounds of Earth and Shell by Bonnie Shemie. A picture book about the mound builders.
	☺ The Ancient Maya by Jackie Maloy.
	☺ ☺ A History of US: vol 1 by Joy Hakim: Though the author relies a great deal on scholarly speculation about unknowns like the timeline of migration and the linear progression from cave man to civilization, this volume is a good description of early people of North America. For middle grades or read-aloud for younger kids.
	☺ ☺ Awesome Ancient Ancestors by Elizabeth Levy. A "Horrible Histories" book, this is funny and informative at the same time. Covers North American history up to 1000 AD.
	☺ ☺ Amazing Maya Inventions You Can Build Yourself by Sheri Bell-Rehwoldt.
	☺ ☺ Secrets in Stone: All About Maya Hieroglyphs by Laurie Coulter. The target audience is really younger kids, but we think middle schoolers will love it too, particularly as you can't find this information written for kids in other places.
	☺ ☺ The Earliest Americans by Helen Roney Sattler. Explores the various theories about the migrations to America. Contains evolutionary and cave-man material.
	☺ The Ancient Maya by Lila Perl.
	☺ Talking Bones: Secrets of Indian Burial Mounds by William O. Steele. Slightly freaky and macabre in places; kids should love it.
	☺ First People by David C. King. The first few chapters of the book cover ancient Americas. The book then moves into the coming of Europeans and the modern condition of the various tribes in North America.
	☺ Ancient Civilizations of the Americas by Antony Mason. From DK, this book covers both North and South America from the most ancient of times clear up until the Age of Exploration.
	☺ ☺ ☺ North American Peoples by Elizabeth Baquedano. Tons of great photos and drawings interspersed with excellent information.
	☺ Exodus Lost by S.C. Compton. Theory of the migration of the ancient Mexican people (Olmec and Maya) from Egypt. Well written, entertaining, and thoroughly researched.

First North Americans – North America – Salts – Creative Kids

GEOGRAPHY	Search for: North America • North America by Libby Koponen • North America by David Petersen. • • The Hispanics by Mark Nickles. Part of the "We Came To North America" series, these books discuss each cultural group who migrated to America, the history behind their move, and where they are today. Check out the whole series. • • Paddle To the Sea by Holling C. Holling. A boy carves a wooden boat that travels down rivers and across half of the North American continent before floating out to sea. • North America: The Historical Geography of a Changing Continent by Thomas F. McIlwraith and Edward K. Muller, et. al. Covers the way the North American continent was mapped, how cultures moved across it, and how the maps and regions changed over time. • Across This Land by John C. Hudson. Used as a text for some college geography courses, this book is written for a lay audience and covers regional geography of Canada and the United States.
SCIENCE	Search for: radioactivity, carbon dating, nuclear decay, salts, Marie Curie • • Marie Curie by Kathleen Krull. • • How To Split the Atom by Hazel Richardson. Takes kids through the history and science of nuclear science. Uses cartoons and simple language to teach about complex ideas. • Marie Curie and Radioactivity by Connie Miller. A graphic biography that will appeal to reluctant readers and make good readers tuck it under the covers to read after lights out. • Madame Curie: A Biography by Eve Curie. Written by the famous scientist's daughter.
THE ARTS	Search for: topics specific to your child's interests and creative pursuits

History: First North Americans

North American people arrived on the continent in various ways. Many probably crossed the Bering Strait from Asia when the sea levels were lower due to the Ice Age. No doubt many more came by boat from the Pacific Isles, Europe, Africa, and Asia. We know that long before Columbus, the Vikings and British fishermen were aware of the Americas. Even before that the Phoenicians were rumored to have made it to the western continent. No doubt through the millennia others had found it as well.

Kincaid Site in Illinois, as imagined by artist Herb Roe, 2004, CC license.

Some of these people settled down and built cities and nations and lived cultured civilized lives, others remained tribal or returned to tribal lifestyles when their civilizations collapsed. The people who lived along the coasts of North America were more likely to live in permanent settlements and farmed as well as hunted. The people of the central plains were mostly nomadic, following the buffalo herds.

Two highly developed civilizations emerged. The first group were the Pueblo people who built great cities in the cliffs. The second were the Adena and Hopewell peoples who lived in the Ohio River Valley. We can see their mounds and have found evidence of their cities, but no written records have been found.

Explanation

Though we have dug Egypt from the White Nile to the Delta, sought the lost city of Troy with great zeal, and treasured and gloried in the artifacts of China, we know next to nothing about the ancient people of North America. We are, in fact, at least 200 years behind the discoveries of Europe, North Africa, and the Far East.

If you would like to see firsthand the confusion, misinformation, and blundering that the early stages of archeological exploration produce, keep an eye on the diggings of the mound people of our own continent. *The builders were the same people as the current Indian tribes . . . no they were different people . . . no one ever migrated over the ocean to the Americas . . . yes they did . . . they borrowed culture from the Celts . . . no the Celts came later.*

It'll help you understand 19th century archeologists a little better.

Michelle

First North Americans – North America – Salts – Creative Kids

The most advanced civilizations are a little further south in Mexico, especially on the Yucatan Peninsula and south of there. The earliest we know of are the Olmecs, followed by the Maya, who built pyramids and great cities of stone carved out of the jungle. We know they farmed and traded with surrounding peoples. We also know they created art and had complex mathematical knowledge and a written language. We can read their writings, but they have been found only as inscriptions on the sides of buildings or monuments, and are therefore limited.

☺ ☺ ☺ **EXPLORATION: Timeline of North America**
All ancient dates are approximate. You will find printable timeline squares at the end of this unit.
- 1200BC - 400 BC Olmec people
- 1000 - 300BC Adena people
- 300 BC - 550 AD Hopewell people
- 300 BC - 900 AD Maya people
- 5000 BC Corn (maize) is systematically bred to resemble modern forms.
- 32 BC Olmecs begin to use zero as a place holder in calculations
- 1000 AD City of Chahokia (near St. Louis) rises
- 1398 AD Tlacaelel born

☺ ☺ **EXPLORATATION: Land Bridge Model**
One theory regarding the migration of ancient people to the Americas involves a land bridge from Asia.

We named this unit "First North Americans," but the truth is we don't know who the first Americans were, where they came from, how they lived, or where they went. There is much speculation about their origins including "genetic proof" for various theories, maps, routes, and so on, but the truth is probably more complex and more reasonable than any single theory.

Alligator Mound, Ohio

Some archaeologists believe the animal represented by the effigy was the "mascot" of the builder's city. Others believe the sites were used as places of refuge. There are many theories, but no one really knows why they were built.

Fabulous Fact
Other land bridges include the isthmus of Panama, The Sinai Peninsula, and a bridge between England and the Netherlands called Doggerland.

First North Americans – North America – Salts – Creative Kids

Fabulous Fact
Though the ancient southwest cultures of the Pueblo people began as much as 5,000 years ago or more, the height of their civilization wasn't until the Middle Ages. We'll cover them in more detail in Year 2, Unit 18.

Additional Layer
Most ancient cultures operated on the basis of city-states instead of empires or nations. Later the idea of taking large tracts of land by conquest entered in. What do you think is a better government model – the city-state or the large nation? Do modern communication and travel make any difference?

Additional Layer
Why do civilizations like the Greeks, Romans, Egyptians, Hopewell, Maya, British Empire and others collapse? Archaeologists like to speculate about natural disasters and conquest having a big roll, but historical evidence of people we know more about usually indicates collapse from within before being destroyed from without.

We began by making homemade salt dough. We shaped it to form two continents that were connected by a slightly lower elevation bridge of land. Next we put a little blue food coloring in some water and poured it until it was just below the land bridge. We put ice cubes throughout, both in the water and on the continents. As the ice melts, it causes the water level to rise and covers the land bridge with "ocean." If you look closely at our land bridge above, you can still see the land under the water in the center. By the end the ice that has melted on the continents also fills in little lakes and looks pretty neat.

🙂 🙂 🙂 **EXPLORATION:** Ancient American Peoples Map

Make a map of ancient American peoples. Use the North America map from the end of this unit. Label and color the homelands for the Olmec, Adena, Hopewell, and Maya people. Note that there were many other tribes and people across the entire continent who we know little about and so are not included on the map.

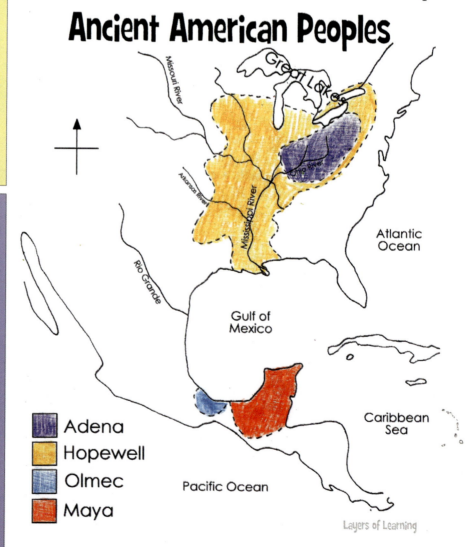

First North Americans – North America – Salts – Creative Kids

😊 😊 😊 **EXPEDITION: Ohio River Valley**

If you live in the Ohio River Valley take a trip to see an ancient burial mound of the Hopewell people. If you can't make it in person look up www.nps.gov/hocu and visit the Hopewell culture over the web.

😊 😊 😊 **EXPLORATION: Four Types of Mounds**

The mound builders of Ohio and the Mississippi River Valley, people we call the Adena and the Hopewell among others, built four types of earthen mounds: conical, platform, geometric, and effigy.

Conical mounds mostly just look like hills, some of them quite large, but most small. A few of the mounds hold burial remains, but most do not, though they do have many artifacts like jewelry, shells, metal tools and so on. It is unclear why these mounds were built.

Conical mounds in Ohio.
Photograph by Heironymous Rowe at en.wikipedia

In the painting by Herb Roe at the beginning of this section you can see houses built on top of platform mounds. When Europeans first encountered woodland tribes of this area some of them were still using platform mounds for the chief's house, temples, dance floors, residences, funeral platforms, and town halls. Archaeologists assume that ancient people used the platform mounds for similar purposes.

Fabulous Facts

The mounds weren't just earth piled up in a heap. They were carefully engineered with specific types of clay and soils being used in specific places so the steep sided mounds wouldn't slump or erode.

Some of the large mounds had smaller mounds on top of them.

When the people built a mound they left a hole behind somewhere else. Sometimes these pits were filled with water and stocked with fish.

Additional Layer

The mound builders often buried their dead in stone boxes, large flat stones lining the sides of an earthen pit. A sacrificial pot, smashed on purpose, would often be added to graves along with valuables like jewelry and tools.

How does this compare to the burial practices of your culture?

Drawing by Herb Roe and shared on Wikimedia commons.

First North Americans – North America – Salts – Creative Kids

On The Web
Visit the National Park Service's site about the mound builders here:

http://www.nps.gov/history/nr/travel/mounds/builders.htm

Fabulous Fact
At one time there were thousands and thousands of human-made mounds all over the Mississippi and Ohio Valley regions. Most of them have been destroyed by farming and the building of cities.

Additional Layer
If you live in the Midwest or along any major river, you know that building out of earth isn't as simple as it sounds. The problem is water.

Sure, earth is easy enough to pile up in a big heap or a long dike, but keeping it there amid rain and river run-off is something else entirely. The fact that so many of the ancient mounds lasted for thousands of years is no mean feat of engineering.

Learn how modern levees are made and compare this to the techniques of the mound builders.

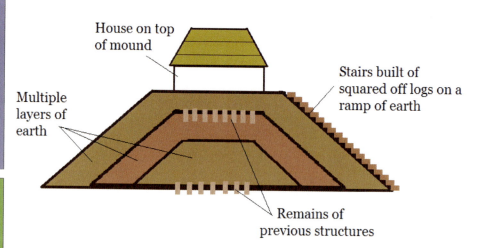

Geometric mounds are really enclosures, like fences built of earth. They surround large areas in rectangles and circles. Perhaps these were important religious or government sites.

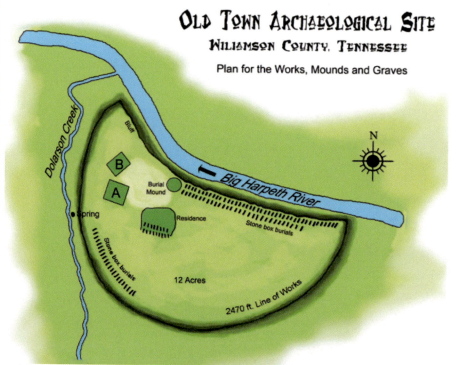

A complex of buildings and grave sites surrounded by a geometric earth mound. Image created by Herb Roe and shared on Wikimedia Commons.

Effigy mounds are built to look like an animal, such as the serpent mound in Ohio. There are no human remains in the mound and so it could not have been a burial mound. Archaeologists speculate that this mound and other effigy mounds were used for religious purposes.

First North Americans – North America – Salts – Creative Kids

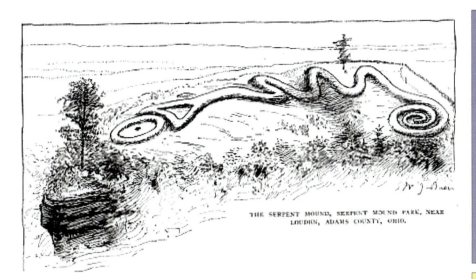

THE SERPENT MOUND, SERPENT MOUND PARK, NEAR LOUDEN, ADAMS COUNTY, OHIO.

Choose one type of mound and build a model of it out of clay, salt dough, earth, or whatever you'd like.

☺ ☺ EXPLORATION: Who Built the Mounds?

In the early days, late 1700's to late 1800's and beyond, there was a great deal of speculation about these mysterious mounds, who built them, and why. Few of the Indian tribes living in the region had any stories or recollections about the mounds. The tribes, as found by the American settlers, were few in number and did not engage in city or monument building of their own. All these reasons led some people to believe that the direct ancestors of these Indians could not have been the same people that built these extensive mounds, which obviously required hard work, cooperation, and a large, dense population. They would have needed farming, social and political stability, and strength.

Read the article "Who Built the Wisconsin Mounds?" found at the end of this unit. The article was published in *The Madison Democrat*, a newspaper, March 25, 1906 by an anonymous author.

In 1855 Increase Laphap, a civil engineer, wrote a long explanation about the mounds found in the upper Mississippi Valley, entitled "The Antiquities of Wisconsin." You can find the whole article online. In his conclusion Laphap puts forth his theory of who built the mounds.

We may, therefore, without assuming any far-fetched theories, suppose that a nation or tribe of red men formerly occupied the country now known as Wisconsin, whose superstitions, ceremonies, and beliefs, required the erection of mounds of earth of the various forms represented on the plates accompanying

---

Additional Layer

A modern art movement called "earthworks" uses natural artifacts to create art directly on the ground. Usually these are rather massive and can be viewed most easily from above. The mound builders of course did this thousands of years before modern artists.

Fabulous Fact

We tend to think of American civilizations as backward compared to their contemporary European counterparts. Certainly some of the civilizations were, but many were actually more advanced than the people who discovered them. They had large complex cities, developed written languages, mathematics, astronomy and other technologies.

Additional Layer

Do you think sites such as these mounds should be preserved? Some of them or all of them? What should be done about mounds already located on private land? Do you think they should be excavated for archeology?

First North Americans – North America – Salts – Creative Kids

Legends

There are legends even older than the two theories presented here. 19th century Indian tribes spoke of a legendary race of giants who lived in the Ohio River Valley. They were known as the Alleg and from their name comes the Allegheny Mountains.

They themselves had come from the west. Then later more people, the Lenape, wanted to settle in the Alleg lands. When the Lenape asked permission they were refused, but were allowed to travel through on their way to more distant eastern lands. When the Alleg saw the many thousands of Lenape settlers they were afraid and decided to attack. A great war ensued and eventually the Alleg were defeated, their bones heaped into pits and covered with earth. The Lenape became the ancestors of the modern northeastern tribes.

*From Henry Schoolcraft

Additional Layer

Sadly, nearly all the old manuscripts preserved from ancient times in the Americas were burned with the coming of the Spanish who viewed all things Indian as heretical.

---

this work; and that these tribes may have emigrated, or been driven off by others having no veneration for their ancient monuments. These subsequent tribes may or may not be the same that until very recently occupied that country. They extended their cultivation over the mounds with as little feeling of respect as is manifested by men of the race who are now fast destroying them. It is quite certain that these later tribes continued the practice of mound-building so far as to erect a circular or conical tumulus over their dead. This practice appears to be a remnant of ancient customs that connects the mound-builders with the present tribes.

The extent of the ancient works in the West indicates a condition of society somewhat different from the purely savage or hunter state: for to accomplish the labor required for the completion of such large structures, it would be necessary to accumulate the means of subsistence; and this could be done only by an agricultural people, or at least agriculture must have been among the pursuits of a people capable of constructing those works. Now we know that nearly all the Indian tribes cultivate the soil to some extent; and is it not reasonable to suppose that the amount of attention devoted to that pursuit may have been greater at former times than at present? A tribe or nation may gradually change its habits in relation to one or another class of pursuits, and yet remain essentially the same people. Again, the Indians are to a certain extent migratory; and hence we may look for the posterity of the mound-builders of Wisconsin in remote portions of the country.

Then discuss:
- What reasons does the first author give for doubt about the builders of the mounds?
- The author of "Who Built the Wisconsin Mounds?" says "No such Indian settlements as we have knowledge of could have built them." Do you agree? Could the Indian people the Americans had "knowledge of" been the builders of the mounds?
- What do you think is required for a society to build major public works, cities, roads, establish trade routes, and so on?
- Brainstorm all the possibilities of who could have built the mounds. Make a list and discuss the scenarios that could have happened to cause this highly organized society to disappear so completely.
- What conclusions did archaeologists come to in regard to the builders of the mounds? What explanation do they give as to the disappearance of this civilization? Do you agree with their conclusions?

First North Americans – North America – Salts – Creative Kids

😊 🟢 EXPLORATION: Olmec Heads

The Olmec were the earliest highly developed civilization in the Americas that we know of. They were at their height at about the same time as ancient Greece. Since archaeologists have found few examples of their writing and it differs from the writing of other nearby cultures, we know little about the Olmec. They appear to have completely died out or perhaps moved at about the same time the later Mayan people were getting underway.

The most distinctive thing about the Olmec is their art. They created many statues out of stone like these giant stone heads. No one in the modern world has any idea of who these stone heads represent or why they were built. Are they portraits of kings? Are they gods that were worshiped? Is there another explanation?

Find the Olmec heartland on a map of Mexico (you can see the location on the map from this unit). Come up with your own story of what these gigantic heads were built for. You can pretend to be a brilliant archeologist, you can pretend to find a firsthand account written by an ancient artist, or you could pretend to be the rich guy or gal who ordered one to be carved. Write down your story.

😊 🟢 ⚫ EXPLORATION: Mayan Place in Society

Make a "class map" of the Mayan culture. Draw a picture representing each of the classes and label it.

Mayans got slaves when they conquered their neighbors in battle. This class structure looks very much like the class structures in Europe, China, and nearly every other society. Why do you think it works out like this? How are modern people the same? Different?

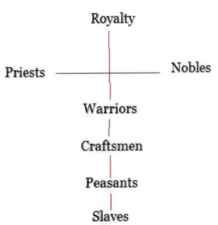

Where Did They Come From?

There's a great deal of speculation about the Olmec art because the people in it have African and Asian as well as Caucasian features, with some tending more toward one modern race than another.

Some say these features were carved because of the shape of the stone and the real people didn't actually look that way at all. Others say the Olmec were Africans who immigrated over the sea and perhaps maintained trade routes for a thousand years.

Most modern archaeologists scoff at the idea of ancient people having the ability to travel over vast oceans, but there is a small core of opposition that says certainly ancient people traveled at least sometimes over the sea.

What do you think?

On The Web

Look up the story of the hero twins for an exciting Mayan myth.

http://mayas.mrdonn.org/herotwins.html

First North Americans – North America – Salts – Creative Kids

The Mesoamerican ball game you've heard tell of is rumored to have started during Olmec times or perhaps even earlier. It is still played in some places today. The ball is solid rubber and very heavy. Players get massive bruises that never quite heal.

Photograph by Manuel Aguilar, CC license

🙂 🟢 EXPLORATION: Mayan Pyramids

There are two different types of Mayan pyramids, though they look very much alike. The first type had a square base and triangular sides meeting at a flat top with a temple at the top. There were stairs leading up one or more sides. These pyramids were used to make offerings to the

Photograph by Manuel de Corselas and shared on Wikimedia commons.

gods and to store stuff like grain. The other type of pyramid looked just the same except it was ceremonial, dedicated to a god, and riddled with false passages and booby traps. The Mayans would have known which was which, but modern archeologists have to tread carefully because they can't tell.

Write an adventure story of the discovery of a Mayan pyramid buried deep in the jungle.

The major deity of many ancient American cultures was the feathered serpent. The feathers represent the ability of the god to fly to the heavens and the serpent represents the ability to descend down to the earth.

🙂 🟢 🔵 EXPLORATION: Pottery Cup

The Maya made beautiful pottery. Make a pottery cup in Mayan style. Use slabs of clay, rolled out flat. Incise designs onto the clay, shape it into a cylinder, then add a circular base. Use your fingers to smooth the base and cylinder sides together before you bake it in the

oven. Once it is baked you can paint it with acrylic paints if you like.

Geography: North America

North America has two sets of mountains running up its east and west coasts, with the western mountains, the Rockies, being the larger range and running the entire length of the continent from upper Canada to southern Mexico. In the central part of the continent are vast stretches of prairie. The mountains to the Mississippi River in the east and the coastal regions are mostly wooded, except in the southwest, which is desert. The largest river system is the Mississippi River drainage basin running up the center of the continent. The northern reaches of the continent give way to a multitude of islands which are claimed mostly by Canada, but also by Russia in some places. The island of Greenland is the largest northern island and is an independent country, under Denmark. In the south, the continent tapers off into a slender isthmus that connects North America to South America. The southern lands are known as Central America. In addition, there are thousands of islands in the Caribbean Sea and Gulf of Mexico. Some animals unique to North America include the bald eagle, prairie dog, porcupine, opossum, raccoon, and many more.

Though people from every place and culture can be found in North America, the population is predominantly of European descent. The two most common languages spoken are English and Spanish. About half the countries have some kind of republican form of government, while the other half have a centralized, controlled form of government. Generally, the northern countries have more freedom than the southern and, not coincidentally, more prosperity as well.

We'll also do a few exploration on time zones in this unit to learn the concept of time across the globe.

☺ ☺ ☺ **EXPLORATION: Political Map of North America**
Label and color the political map of North America. Include the countries and the capitals including the islands of the Caribbean. Use a student atlas as a guide.

☺ ☺ ☺ **EXPLORATION: North American Map**
Color a physical map of the North American continent. We provide a printable map at the end of this unit. Use a student atlas or a globe to find some or all of these features (the amount you label will depend on how old your kids are):

On the Web
Read purely North American folk stories at www.Americanfolklore.net.
They have Canadian, American, and Mexican stories from ancient times to modern urban legends.

Additional Layer
Arctic wolves live in the very far northern reaches of North America. They prey on muskox, arctic hare, caribou, seals, lemmings, arctic birds, and more.

The Grizzly Bear is an American subspecies of the brown bear.

First North Americans – North America – Salts – Creative Kids

Additional Layer

Go off on a tangent – Learn about the lighthouses of North America (U.S. and Canada), coastal geography, the science behind the light, what it's like to live in a lighthouse and more in a hands-on activity book called *Lighthouses of North America* by Lisa Trumbaouer.

Or if your kid is a sports fanatic read about soccer all over the continent in *Soccer in North America* by Mike Kennedy.

Then of course there's the adventurous kid who craves monster stories. For her we offer *Monster Spotter's Guide to North America* by Scott Francis, a complete compendium of local legends from the natives to the moderns from the Arctic Circle to the Yucatan Peninsula and beyond.

A New Way To Look

What if the political boundaries on the map had turned out differently? Make new country borders and name your countries.

Islands and Coastal Features:
- Aleutian Islands
- Greenland
- Newfoundland
- Greater Antilles
- Lesser Antilles
- Yucatan Peninsula
- Baja Peninsula
- Panama Isthmus

Rivers and Lakes:
- Rio Grande
- Mississippi River
- St. Lawrence River
- Colorado River
- Lake Nicaragua
- Great Lakes
- Lake Winnipeg
- Great Slave Lake
- Great Bear Lake
- Great Salt Lake

Seas:
- Atlantic Ocean
- Pacific Ocean
- Arctic Ocean
- Gulf of Mexico
- Caribbean Sea
- Gulf of Alaska
- Hudson Bay
- Labrador Sea
- Beaufort Sea
- Bering Sea
- Bering Strait

Mountains:
- Rocky Mountains
- Appalachian Mountains
- Sierra Madre Mountains
- Laurentian Mountains

Others:
- Great Plains
- Sonoran Desert
- Tropic of Cancer
- Arctic Circle
- North Pole

EXPLORATION: Grand Canyon

Find the Grand Canyon on a map of North America. You may want to add several of the landmarks found in the next explorations to a map of North America (from the end of this unit). Make a poster of the Grand Canyon including pictures you print out or draw. Include captions describing the pictures. Consider including animals found at the Grand Canyon, a map showing how to get there from your town, natural features like the Colorado River, Bright Angel Creek, or the strata in the walls, and a diagram of how the canyon was formed.

EXPLORATION: Niagara Falls

Find Niagara Falls on a map of North America. Now have your kids make up a board game including a trip down the river through the falls and to the Atlantic Ocean. You can find another Niagara Falls exploration and more activities at http://www.layers-of-learning.com/niagaras-trickle/

EXPLORATION: Yellowstone National Park

Find Yellowstone National Park on a map of North America. Then visit www.windowsintowonderland.org to take an e-field trip produced by the National Park Service.

First North Americans – North America – Salts – Creative Kids

😊 😊 😊 EXPLORATION: The Everglades

Find the Florida Everglades on a map of North America. The everglades are really just a big grassy swampy swamp. But they provide important functions in water drainage and wildlife habitat. Learn how the Everglades became a national park. Make a timeline. Use pictures printed from the Internet to illustrate your timeline. The gator above was one we met on one of our airboat trips to the Everglades.

😊 😊 😊 EXPLORATION: Dancers

Compare the two photographs of native dancers from the end of this unit. The boy in purple and black is an Aztec dancer from Mexico City. The boy in red and yellow is a Native American dancer from San Diego, USA. Ask the kids to look at the two photos and pick out cultural differences and similarities. They should notice things like indoor or outdoor, skin/hair color, differences and similarities in the costumes, and people and objects in the background. You can expand this by finding other similar photos of two different places. Like a city park in Toronto and one in Seattle, or a church in Phoenix and one in Cuba, or the skyline of New York compared to Guadalajara.

😊 😊 EXPLORATION: Mexico City

Find Mexico City on a map of North America. Mexico City, one of the largest cities in the world, is built on the site of an ancient shallow lake.

The only remaining portion of that lake is in a neighborhood in Mexico City called Xochimilco. If you go there you will find flower gardens and floating vegetation interspersed with pleasure boats. Vendors and flower girls crowd the sidewalks and the waterways with tourists and locals.

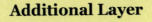
Xochimilco Gardens with the distinctive boats from the lake. Photograph by Clinker, CC license.

Make a model of the Xochimilco boats. Use paper french fry boats, and construction paper to make the distinctive shapes.

Additional Layer

The other grand canyon of North America lies in Mexico.

It is called Copper Canyon and is deeper and larger than the Grand Canyon of Arizona.

Learn more about the canyon: http://www.visitmexico.com/en/copper-canyon

Additional Layer

Other map activities:

Map the locations of your child's ten favorite sports teams.

Look up and map the top fifteen largest cities in North America.

Map ten places you would like to visit in North America.

Make a map of literary sites, where books take place . . . don't forget our favorite: Prince Edward Island.

First North Americans – North America – Salts – Creative Kids

Fabulous Fact

Pronghorns, endemic to North America and famously mentioned in the American Classic "Home On The Range" as antelope are the second fastest land animal in the world. But unlike the faster cheetah, pronghorns can run at 60 miles per hour for hours on end.

Fabulous Fact

The muskox is a North American arctic animal with a strong smell, hence the name.

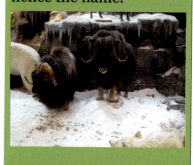

Additional Layer

Do you agree with the choice of presidents to represent America on Mount Rushmore? Would you pick someone else or someone in addition? Why?

☺ ☺ EXPLORATION: Mt. Rushmore & Hall of Records

Find Mt. Rushmore on a map of North America. Mt. Rushmore is a giant monument carved, mostly using dynamite, into the side of the mountain. It represents four presidents, George Washington, Thomas Jefferson, Abraham Lincoln, and Teddy Roosevelt, who the artist, John Borglum, felt represented the first 150 years of the nation's history. Behind the monument a special rock chamber was hollowed out to serve as a hall of records to store national documents and treasures, but it was never completed and never filled.

"Carve" your own Mt. Rushmore from chocolate. First make a mold from clay, use new clay so it will be clean. Press four coins, quarter, nickel, dime, and penny into the clay for the faces of the four presidents. Make sure the faces are the side pressed into the clay. Then pour melted chocolate into the mold and let it cool. There's not a coin with Teddy on it so we substituted his cousin Franklin. Point it out to the kids to avoid confusion.

☺ ☺ EXPLORATION: Banff National Park

Find Banff National Park on a map of North America. Winning for outright beauty, this park in Alberta is the site of the Chateau Lake Louise, the famous hot springs, lots of mountaineering and skiing as well as summer hiking and recreation.

Banff, Alberta, Canada looking toward Cascade Mountain. Photograph by Diderot and shared on Wikimedia Commons.

Visit www.Banff.ca, the official website of the town of Banff and plan a vacation there. Write up your itinerary and the things you would like to see.

First North Americans – North America – Salts – Creative Kids

☺ ● **EXPLORATION: New York City**
Find New York on a map of North America. Use the New York skyline worksheet from the end of this unit. Color the buildings. If you like you can mount it on cardboard and cut it out. Look at the skylines of several other major North American cities. How are they distinctive?

☺ ● **EXPLORATION: Mexico**
Find Mexico on a Map of North America. Color the map you find at the end of this unit according to the key. Color the oceans and the neighboring countries. Cut the map into several large pieces to make a puzzle then practice putting it together.

☺ ● **EXPLORATION: Animals of North America**
Go online and find some animals that are unique to North America. Here are some unique North American animals:

Roseate Spoonbill	Peccary
Jaguarondi	American Paddlefish
Loggerhead shrike	Trumpeter Swan
Great Horned Owl	Raccoon
Skunk	Pronghorn Antelope

Print out a map of North America from the printables and a small picture of each animal. Mark the location of each of these animals on the map. Place the pictures of the animals around the map with a line drawn from each animal to its habitat. Create a powerpoint slideshow about North American animals.

☺ ● ● **EXPLORATION: Foods of North America**
Try one of these recipes from different countries in North America or have a whole North American banquet.

Additional Layer

Other North American landmarks to take note of:

Mammoth Caves, Tennessee, USA

Confederation Bridge, P.E.I.

Parliament Hill, Ottowa

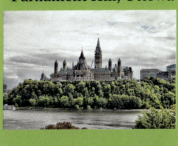

New York, New York

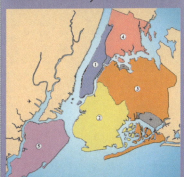

The five boroughs of New York City:

1. Manhattan (blue)
2. Brooklyn (yellow)
3. Queens (orange)
4. The Bronx (pink)
5. Staten Island (purple)

First North Americans – North America – Salts – Creative Kids

Additional Layer

America gets a bad rap for its food. First of all, nearly everything we eat is a rip off from another country. Secondly, the main features of American food involve breading, frying, and lots of cheese. And yet it's American restaurants that can be found all over the world. So besides the classic burger here are some totally American foods:

- Coney Island Hot Dogs
- Corn bread
- "Chinese Food" (The Chinese do not eat double breaded and fried chicken smothered in sugary sauces.)
- Fajitas (from Texas, not Mexico)
- Baked Alaska
- Pizza (Again, this only very remotely resembles its Italian ancestor)
- Chocolate Chip Cookies
- Fried Chicken
- New England Clam Chowder
- Philly Cheese Steak Sandwiches

Famous Folks

American Augustus Jackson particularly deserves our gratitude and thanks as the inventor of the modern method of ice cream manufacture.

Corn Pancakes and Maple Syrup (Canada)
- 1 cup flour
- 1 Tbsp. baking powder
- 1 cup milk
- 2 eggs
- ¼ cup cooking oil
- ½ cup corn

Mix everything in a large mixing bowl until smooth. Heat a greased griddle over medium heat on your stove top. Pour out batter onto the hot griddle in ¼ c. amounts so they form circles. When the top has formed bubbles, flip and cook the other side for another minute. Repeat until all the pancakes are done. Top with real maple syrup.

Cheeseburger (America)
- ¼ pound of ground beef for each burger
- slice of cheddar cheese
- bun

Shape the ground beef into a patty and fry in a skillet or barbecue on a grill, flipping halfway. Place the cheese on while the burger is still on the heat so the cheese melts. Place the cooked patty on a bun. Top with your choice of lettuce, pickles, relish, onions (raw or cooked), ketchup, mustard, cooked bacon and mayonnaise.

Enchiladas (Mexico)
- Small corn tortillas
- tomato sauce
- 6 dried chiles
- 1 tsp. salt
- 1 clove garlic
- filling of cooked chopped chicken or beef and crumbled queso fresco

Prepare the sauce by chopping the peppers finely and adding them along with the salt and diced garlic to the tomato sauce.

Dip each tortilla into the sauce then fry in hot oil on a griddle for a just a few seconds on each side. Stack on a plate until you have cooked all your tortillas. Then place hot filling inside each tortilla and roll up, placing them seam side down onto a serving dish. Serve with re-fried beans, sour cream, and guacamole.

First North Americans – North America – Salts – Creative Kids

Jamaican Jerked Meat (Jamaica)
First make your blend of Jamaican spices:
- 1 tsp. onion, finely chopped
- 3 Tbsp. brown sugar
- 2 tsp. thyme
- 3 cloves garlic, diced
- 1 hot pepper (habanero or another hot variety)
- ½ tsp. allspice
- 1 tsp. cooking oil (coconut oil is amazing in this recipe)

Blend these ingredients all together in a food processor until smooth. Place in a zippered plastic bag with four pieces of chicken, pounded flat with a meat mallet, to marinate for at least an hour in the refrigerator. Remove the chicken from the marinade and broil in the oven for 10 minutes on each side or until done. Alternatively, you can grill the chicken over flame.

Heat the remaining marinade in a small sauce pan with 1 cup chicken broth until it boils to serve over the chicken. Serve with black beans and rice and fresh tropical fruits.

☺ ☺ ☻ EXPLORATION: Melting Pot

America has been called a melting pot because people from every culture and location on Earth have come to this continent in search of freedom and economic prosperity. Altogether the unique cultures of North America are an amalgamation of the world cultures that made them up. North American nations are nations of immigrants. Most of the inhabitants have ancestors that immigrated (or were brought) to the continent in the last three hundred years or so.

Make bar graphs representing the various cultures that have come together on the North American continent.

Religion:
Christian 83% (Mexico is about 97% Christian)
Islam 1% (by far the largest number of Muslims live in Canada)
Judaism 1%
Non-religious 12%
Buddhism .5%
Hinduism .5%
Other 2%

Languages:
Spanish 35%
English 46%
French 8%
Native 2.5%
Indian .5%
Chinese .9%
Other 7.1%

Memorization Station

The poem by Emma Lazarus that is engraved on the Statue of Liberty aptly describes the way America has functioned as a refuge for immigrants since the pilgrims first fled to America.

The New Colossus

Not like the brazen giant of Greek fame,

With conquering limbs astride from land to land;

Here at our sea-washed, sunset gates shall stand

A mighty woman with a torch, whose flame

Is the imprisoned lightning, and her name

Mother of Exiles. From her beacon-hand

Glows world-wide welcome; her mild eyes command

The air-bridged harbor that twin cities frame.

"Keep ancient lands, your storied pomp!" cries she

With silent lips. "Give me your tired, your poor,

Your huddled masses yearning to breathe free,

The wretched refuse of your teeming shore.

Send these, the homeless, tempest-tost to me,

I lift my lamp beside the golden door!"

First North Americans – North America – Salts – Creative Kids

Additional Layer

Learn about daylight savings time. Who uses it? Who doesn't? Why do some countries and states have daylight savings time while others do not?

Origin Country/ Ethnic Groups:
British Isles 4.6%
French 6.2%
German 8.1%
Irish 8%
Italian 3.4%
Chinese .72%
Ukrainian 1.2%
Native 6.8%
Canadian/American/ Mexican 17.8%
Mixed 20.3%
Spanish 3%
African 3%
Polish 1%
Other 4.5%

☺ ☻ EXPLORATION: Greenwich

The official "zero" time zone is Greenwich, England. All other time zones are plus or minus Greenwich time. Use a timezone map in your student atlas to count how many time zones away you are from Greenwich, England. Are you behind Greenwich or ahead? When it is midnight in Greenwich, what time is it where you live?

☺ ☻ EXPLORATION: Timezone Map

There are 24 time zones all together. One for each hour of the day. You can print out a timezone map from the U.S. Naval Observatory online at
http://aa.usno.navy.mil/faq/docs/world_tzones.php

☺ ☻ EXPLORATION: Time Zone Clock

Make a time zone clock. Purchase four clock hand sets. Paint a piece of 12"x4' wood (any type you like) in any color you like. Let it dry completely. Then using a template (a dinner plate works well) or a compass, make four circles equidistant apart and in a row. The four circles will be the faces of the clocks. Drill a hole in the exact center of each circle for your clock parts to go through. Label the first clock after your city and set it to your local time. Pick three more cities in different time zones around the world. Traditionally this type of clock will show the times for big important financial centers like Tokyo, New York, Paris and so on, but you can pick any place you like. Set each of the clocks to their time zone. You can decorate the board in any way you like.

Additional Layer

Modern text books and teacher lesson plans call the melting pot a myth and instead insist that America is a tossed salad.

Of course definitions are important. Generally a melting pot implies that many cultures have come together to create a unifying culture. The tossed salad metaphor implies that many different and distinct cultures are living side by side, but not really mixing.

Which do you think is true? Was one true in the past and one true now? Is one more desirable than another? What are the problems and benefits for a nation under each method? Which societal structure do you think is best for a nation in order to create stability, culture, prosperity, and peace within the borders? Are these the only two choices?

☺ ☻ EXPLORATION: International Date Line

Not only do we have official time zones but we also have official worldwide dates these days. In the middle of the Pacific there is an imaginary line that runs from the south pole to the north pole. This is the International Date Line. On one side of the line it is one day and on the other it's already tomorrow. Use a globe to see if you can figure out if Hawaii is the last place to see a day go or the first.

Science: Radioactivity and Salts

Most atoms are stable and do not change, but some lose particles from their nucleus. When they do, we say they are radioactive. A common radioactive atom is uranium. When an atom loses a neutron and has a different atomic mass we call it an isotope. Uranium 238 (meaning it has 238 neutrons and protons) loses parts of its nucleus, making an isotope, then it begins to really fall apart and changes its nature entirely, becoming a lead isotope as particles for the nucleus go charging off and electrons go zooming around. Uranium loses two neutrons and two protons at a time. There are three types of radiation: alpha, beta and gamma. Alpha rays are parts of the nucleus and are not very harmful. Beta rays are electrons, and aren't terribly dangerous either. Gamma rays are electromagnetic radiation, the really dangerous stuff that attacks and destroys your cells.

Radioactivity isn't all bad though. We use radiation in smoke alarms, pacemakers, cancer treatments, power production, industry and more. The carbon 14 isotope can be used to date things that contain carbon. In any bit of carbon, normally containing 12 protons and neutrons, there are some carbon atoms that have 2 extra neutrons, the carbon-14 isotope. The carbon 14 decays at a known rate, called the half-life. A half life is the time it takes for half of the carbon in a sample to decay. So if you find a dead stick in the woods and want to know how old it is you could do carbon-14 testing to find out. But whatever you test has to have carbon in it and generally only things that are alive or were once alive have carbon in them. So you can't test old pottery or rocks or mineralized fossils using carbon-14.

Salts are metal and non-metal elements joined together in an ionic bond. So sodium and bromine could join together to form a salt and so could lithium and fluorine, but carbon and oxygen joined will not a salt make. Salts generally dissolve easily in water, they usually form crystals, and they are produced when acids and bases react. Very little of the earth's water is free of salt because it dissolves so easily. And that is a good thing for you, because your body needs those dissolved salts to function.

Famous Folks

Lise Meitner, along with her partner, Otto Hahn, discovered nuclear fission.

Additional Layer

X-rays and gamma rays are the same thing, different names. Remember how Superman has x-ray vision, but can't see through lead? Gamma rays can't pass through lead. Make up your own x-ray using superhero. What can he or she do with those powerful x-rays?

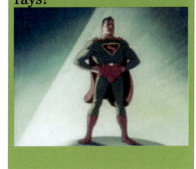

First North Americans – North America – Salts – Creative Kids

Additional Layer

Uranium and Thorium decay are the major sources of energy that keep the center of the earth hot.

Famous Folks

The Geiger counter is named for its inventor, Hans Geiger. Besides creating a device to detect radiation he also co-discovered the atomic nucleus.

He was born in Germany in 1882 and died just after the end of World War II. He worked with Ernest Rutherford and his work aided in Rutherford's model of the atom.

Additional Layer

Find out what happens to radioactive waste after people are done with it. How long does it remain hazardous? What have been the real effects on the environment?

☺ ☺ ☺ EXPERIMENT: Geiger Counter

See if you can arrange to borrow a Geiger counter from a high school or university near you. They may let you use it in the building with supervision if they won't let you take it home. An enthusiastic physicist or chemist may teach you much more than you could learn on your own anyway. The least expensive Geiger counters are well over $150, so you won't want to purchase one just for this unit.

Read background radiation levels in these places:
- inside your home
- outside your home
- near your smoke detector
- wipe dust from an electronic device with a tissue and read the radiation from that
- at 10,000 feet in an airplane if you get the chance
- in the neighborhood of a nuclear power plant, if you live near enough to one
- in front of your microwave while it is running.
- in a cloud of nicotine smoke or where nicotine smoke has recently been.

Keep a table of your findings. Which places have the most radiation? The least?

Inside a building radiation can sometimes become trapped, raising levels slightly. Outside should be low radiation. Your smoke detector may have americum, a low level radioactive isotope in it. Dust collects radioactive particles which you may then breathe in. You skin protects you from most normal low levels of radiation, but your internal organs have no protection. The earth's atmosphere blocks most of the radiation from space, but high up there's not enough atmosphere to do the job. Nicotine smoke doesn't produce radiation, but radioactive particles are attracted to it, and when you breathe them in . . .

☺ ☺ EXPERIMENT: Radon Tester

Radon gas commonly occurs naturally in soil from Uranium-238. Get an inexpensive radon testing kit for your house to see if it's a problem where you live. Do some research to find out how the kit works. Oddly enough, it's not the radon that is the problem, but the things that radon decays into; first, polonium, then lead. These things get attracted to dust in your home and you breathe them in.

First North Americans – North America – Salts – Creative Kids

☺ ☺ ☺ **EXPEDITION: Virtual Ping Pong Reactions**
There are some pretty cool videos on You Tube of ping-pong ball chain reactions. They demonstrate the way a nuclear chain reaction works. Shoot a positron or a neutrino at a nucleus and you speed up the decomposition of the nucleus. That nucleus sends out more particles which hit other nuclei and pretty soon, you have a pretty good reaction going on.

☺ **EXPLORATION: Half-Life**
Radioactive elements have what is called a half-life. A half-life is the time it takes for half of the atoms in a sample to decompose. Some very radioactive elements have very short half-lives, mere seconds or less. Others aren't so unstable and have much longer half-lives, days, weeks, or even years. Learn more about half-lives at Khan Academy. Watch the first two videos on the list.
https://www.khanacademy.org/science/chemistry/radioactive-decay
Then complete the half-life worksheet from the end of this unit.

☺ ☺ **EXPERIMENT: Salts Conduct Electricity**
You need a beaker (or glass) filled with salt water. A second beaker filled with plain tap water, electric wire, a D cell battery (or four AA), and a flashlight light bulb. Build an apparatus similar to the one below:

Tim built this apparatus using Snap Circuits, but you don't need this "toy," just break out the electric wire and some masking tape to keep your connections in place.

Famous Folks
Read about Marie Curie, the scientist who discovered radioactivity.

Fabulous Fact
Radon has always come from the soil, but it wasn't a problem until we developed such awesomely weather proof houses. The lack of air flow to the outside means that harmful gases like radon can get trapped inside.

Additional Layer
You've probably seen sports drinks that promise they provide electrolytes. Electrolytes are salts dissolved in solution that conduct electricity. This is important to your body because electrolytes conduct signals from the brain to your body and help muscles relax and contract.

First North Americans – North America – Salts – Creative Kids

Definitions

When you dissolve a substance in water you are creating a solution.

The dissolver is called the solvent.

The substance dissolved is called the solute.

In salt water solution the water is the solvent and the salt is the solute.

If you put in so much salt that no more can dissolve in it, we say the solution is saturated.

It's A Funny

A young chemistry student runs into the lab holding a beaker of liquid and excitedly says to his professor, "I've got it! The universal solvent!"

The professor calmly answers, "Is that it in the glass beaker? And why isn't the glass dissolving?"

Okay, so it's only funny if you're a chemistry nerd.

A "universal solvent," or a solvent that dissolves everything, is one of the holy grails of chemistry. Water does a pretty good job of dissolving a multitude of solutes and is probably the closest we'll ever come, but it's far from universal.

Connect the wire to the battery while in the salt solution and see if the light bulb comes on. Test it in the plain water solution as well.

In order for a substance to conduct electricity it must have free ions, or positive and negative charges, floating around in it. Salts, because of their ionic bonds (see Unit 1-14), have positive and negatively charged particles. In a liquid, when the salt is dissolved, some of the molecules dissociate into ions which can move around and flow. The flowing of charges is electricity.

☺ ☻ **EXPERIMENT: Separating The Salt From The Sand**

In a bowl or plastic bag, mix sand and table salt together in roughly equal amounts, exactness is unimportant in this experiment. Then ask your kids to separate the sand from the salt. Brainstorm ways to do this.

Salts are soluble, that is, they dissolve in water. Dissolving means the water can break apart the crystalline structure (for more on crystals see Unit 1-14) and you get individual molecules of NaCl floating around plus a fair amount of Na^+ and Cl^- ions.

So to separate sand (non-soluble) from salt (soluble), just add water.

1. Place ¼ c. of the salt and sand mixture in a beaker or glass jar. Add 1 cup hot tap water.
2. Stir well.
3. Prepare a strainer by folding a coffee filter into quarters, unfolding one edge and placing into a funnel, so that the coffee filter covers the inside of the whole funnel.
4. Pour the salt and sand mixture through the funnel. The sand will become trapped in the filter and funnel, but salt water will pass through the filter into a vessel waiting

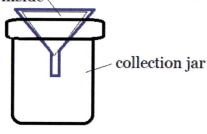

First North Americans – North America – Salts – Creative Kids

below.
5. Pour the salt water into a small sauce pan. Heat on the stove until the water boils off. There should be salt left behind on the bottom and sides of the pan.
6. Measure the amount of salt and sand you have now. Added together does it equal the amount you started with? Why or why not?

😊 🟢 EXPERIMENT: Solubility
You need two beakers or glass jars, water, and table salt.

Measure exactly 1 cup of water into each beaker. One beaker should be filled with cold and the other should be hot.

Add salt to the water 1 teaspoon at a time, stirring as you go, until you can add no more salt. Which beaker of water can hold more salt?

Repeat your experiment using different types of salts: Epsom salts (magnesium sulfate), washing soda (sodium carbonate), rock salt. You may also wish to try it with different types of water: distilled, filtered, spring water, and so on.

😊 🟢 🔵 EXPLORATION: Bath Salts
Bath salts are made using one of three common salts: washing soda (sodium carbonate), table salt (sodium chloride), or Epsom salts (magnesium sulfate).

- 1 c. of sea salt, washing soda, or Epsom salts
- a few drops of essential oil (mint, orange, lavender, etc.)
- food coloring if desired

Pour the salt into a zip-top plastic bag and break up all the lumps. You can run a rolling pin over it to help. Then just add in a few drops of essential oil and food coloring if you want it colored. Knead the salt mixture in the bag thoroughly. Place a few spoonfuls into your hot bath water to try it out.

Bath salts are supposed to improve the cleaning ability of the soap you normally use and also give a nice fragrance to the bath. They don't actually condition your skin or add any nutrients to your skin, even if a company claims that they do. Minerals are not absorbed through your skin, they are only absorbed when you ingest them. But we don't recommend drinking your bath water.

😊 🟢 🔵 EXPERIMENT: Salt Affects Living Things
Slice a potato and place a slice or two into a bowl with saltwater.

Additional Layer

Did you know salt is added to processed meats like lunch meat or hot dogs to make it stick together better? You can try it out by putting ground beef, a little water and salt, ½ tsp. at a time, into a food processor. Mix it up then test the stickiness by throwing the meat at a wall covered with paper. When it sticks, it's done.

Explanation

Kids aren't very often asked to come up with their own experiment design. The first time I was faced with this problem was during my senior year of college when I had to do original research in my field. I totally freaked out. Somehow we've taught our kids how to do everything but think. So whenever we can, we put in an experiment that kids have to design themselves. We also ask good questions without providing the answers. A great education provides some of the answers and models proper results, but also allows for creativity, research, and discovery.

Michelle

First North Americans – North America – Salts – Creative Kids

Additional Layer

The best way to use the lowered freezing point of saltwater is in making homemade ice cream.

Place ½ c. whole milk, 1 T. sugar, and ¼ t. vanilla in a sandwich size zippered bag.

Now fill a gallon size zipper bag ½ full of ice cubes and add 6 T. rock salt. Put the small bag inside the large bag and toss it around until the milk is frozen.

Fabulous Facts

Washing soda is used in laundry soaps to aid the soap in doing its job of cleaning. Washing soda is also used in industry and glass making.

Epsom salts can be taken internally as a laxative. Most people use Epsom salts to soak their feet in or as an additive to their bath water where it has the same effect as an aid in cleaning as the washing soda does. It's also supposed to be good for bruises or minor sprains.

Place another slice or two of potato into a bowl with plain water. Let it sit for an hour or two. Go back and feel the potatoes. The salty water pulls water out of the potato cells because water wants to have the same saturation of salt throughout. That's why you can't drink a lot of saltwater without it killing you. The saltwater pulls water out of your cells.

☺ ☺ ☻ **EXPERIMENT: Salts and the Freezing Point**

Design an experiment to test if saltwater freezes at the same temperature as fresh water. Remember to use the scientific method. First come up with a hypothesis, or educated guess about how you think the salt will affect the water freezing point. Next, design an experiment with a control. A control is a neutral test subject that you can use to compare to your test subject. Then keep track of your data. For example, check your water temperature every minute or so and record it. Then write up your results with graphs and charts as needed. What are your conclusions?

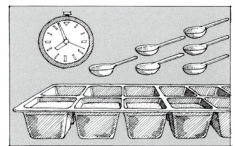

You might try this with salt and the boiling temperature of water as well.

☺ ☻ **EXPERIMENT: Salt Precipitation**

Not all salts are soluble in water. In this experiment we're going to mix two soluble salts together and the new salt formed will come out, or precipitate out, of solution.

You need sodium carbonate (washing soda, found in the laundry aisle of the grocery store) and magnesium sulfate (Epsom salts found in the pharmacy area).

1. Prepare a solution of sodium carbonate and water by mixing 1 T. sodium carbonate in 1 c. water in a clean glass jar or flask. If your solution ends up saturated, pour off the top portion into another vessel and let it sit for a minute to get clear.
2. Prepare a solution of magnesium sulfate by mixing 1 T. magnesium sulfate in 1 c. water in a clean glass jar or flask. This one also needs to be clear, so pour off the top portion if you end up with a saturated solution.
3. Pour the two solutions together and stir or swirl to mix. Notice how a white substance appears in the liquid.
4. Carefully pour the solution through a prepared filter

First North Americans – North America – Salts – Creative Kids

funnel (see the filter and funnel apparatus in the following photo).
5. The flask should collect a clear solution.
6. Remove the filter paper from the funnel and lay out carefully to dry. Label it with the date and, if more than one student is doing the experiment, your name.

Make a funnel filter by folding a coffee filter into quarters and opening up into the inside of the funnel.

Pour the solution slowly through the funnel filter so that the solution never goes over the top edge of the filter paper.

Additional Layer

Scientists in Singapore have learned how to pack more electronic bits into the same amount of storage space. They do it by placing the bits in neater patterns. They always understood the principle of neat storage, but the problem was they couldn't see what they were doing. Adding table salt to the mixture during processing made the image of the bits pop out so they could see where the bits were going and pack their bits in neatly.

Additional Layer

Some people buy sea salt to add to their food instead of good old plain table salt. This is because the salt in the sea has many more minerals and nutrients that are essential for the body.

Fabulous Fact

Salts, usually sodium chloride or calcium chloride or a mixture of the two, are often used to clear the ice off roads in places where snow is common. Find out how salts work. Calcium chloride's chemistry is especially cool.

First North Americans – North America – Salts – Creative Kids

The equation for this experiment looks like this:

Sodium carbonate + magnesium sulfate → sodium sulfate + magnesium carbonate

$$Na_2CO_3(aq) + MgSO_4(aq) \rightarrow Na_2SO_4(aq) + MgCO_3(s)$$

aq = aqueous and means the molecule is dissolved in water. s = solid and means the molecule is solid, in this case the magnesium carbonate has precipitated out of solution.

Point out how the names of the salts have swapped partners. For some kids a visual here will be helpful. You can write each part of the names "sodium," "carbonate," "magnesium," and "sulfate" on index cards twice each. Then kids can manipulate the cards around to show how the salts swapped partners. Looking at the chemical equation, can you see which salt precipitated out and ended up on the filter paper and which one stayed in solution?

Boil off most of the water from the solution (don't let it go completely dry) and allow both the filter paper and rest of the water from the solution to evaporate to form salt crystals once again.

EXPLANATION: Salts on the Periodic Table

Take a look at the periodic table. Salts are made of elements on the right hand side joined up with elements from the left side.

Sodium chloride is yellow. Magnesium sulfate is in blue, and potassium bromide is in red.

> **Additional Layer**
>
> Try floating an egg in water. Now add salt and try again. What happens? Do some research and find out why salt affects buoyancy.

> **Additional Layer**
>
> Too much salt in your body will kill you as the water is sucked out of your cells. But too little salt in your body will also kill you as your cells will fill with water and burst.
>
> And did you know that drinking too much water without added salts can kill you. It's called hyponatremia.
>
> Balance, as in the rest of life, is essential.

> **Additional Layer**
>
> Canning and refrigeration have only been around for about a hundred years. Before that people used salt to preserve much of their food, especially meat.
>
> What about salt would prevent food from spoiling?

The Arts: Creative Kids

This unit is different than every other art unit. Rather than focusing on historical art appreciation, principles of art, artists, and skills, the emphasis here is on creativity. So much of what we teach is directed. We ask kids to imitate what we are doing; this is a great way to learn things, but it doesn't teach original thought or creativity. In one unit of each year, we'll ask kids to become songwriters, inventors, and artists in their own right. This exact same unit will appear during one unit in each of the four years, but each time their projects should be new, unique, completely decided upon by the child. Here are ten creativity boosters to choose from:

☺ ☺ ☺ EXPLORATION: Sing Me A Song
Using either your voice or an instrument, write an original song. Write it down, practice it, and plan a performance among your family or peers. For more musically advanced students, you can download Finale Notepad, music notation software, to create printed sheet music. It's inexpensive and really easy to use. You can find it at www.finalemusic.com.

☺ ☺ EXPLORATION: Sell It To Me
Your job is to create a commercial. You can use a real product or create your own new product. Write your script, complete with stage directions. Consider things like costumes, background music, and your scenery. Get some friends to help act in the commercial with you. You'll also need a camera man. Tape the commercial.

EXPLANATION: Buy Bottomless Baggies Today!
Don't feel inhibited by realism or practicality as you create. When I was a teen I created a commercial for a ridiculous product of my own design called "Bottomless Baggies." They were Ziploc bags with the bottoms cut out of them. During the commercial we poured box after box of cereal (and even some milk!) into them, and my goodness, they never filled up! We had a full scene set up and even wrote a jingle. The product was silly and useless, but the creative process that helped bring it all together has stayed with me.

☺ ☺ ☺ EXPLORATION: Tell A Tale
Write your own story about an inanimate object. Imagine you are

---

Famous Folks

Lots of kids become singing stars. Here are some:

- Charlotte Church
- Tanya Tucker
- Gayla Peevey
- Jimmy Boyd
- Lulu
- Frankie Lymon
- Stevie Wonder
- Charice Pempengo
- Micheal Jackson
- Jackie Evancho

Look up one or two of these singers on You Tube to watch them as children.

But you don't have to be famous to use your singing talents for good and you don't have to be a great singer to develop and enjoy your talent.

Brainstorm other ways to use singing to bless your life and the lives of others.

On The Web

Kids can visit www.inventnow.org, a social networking site just for inventor kids. They can post their inventions, comment on other kids inventions, and learn how the patent process works.

First North Americans – North America – Salts – Creative Kids

Explanation

Part of invention and talent is being able to present the great things you've done to other people. Have your kids practice introducing their song or show or explain their invention in front of you. Give them tips like looking at the audience, speaking loudly enough to be heard, standing up straight and not rambling. Then have them present their talent to a bigger audience, like the whole family, grandma and grandpa, or friends.

Famous Folks

Philo T. Farnsworth was fourteen when he made his first prototype of the television.

a pencil, a bar of soap, a space shuttle, a pirate's cannonball – whatever you'd like! Give life and a voice to your object and tell your tale. Make a finished book, complete with illustrations, an about the author page, and of course, a dedication.

☺ ☻ EXPLORATION: Puppeteer

Write your own puppet show. Create your own story, or take an old story and write it with a new twist. You might change the characters, the setting, or the time period. Along with the script, you'll need to create puppets. These could be paper bag puppets, sock puppets, some that you sew, or you could make marionettes. You may need to recruit helpers.

You may want to make your own puppet theater as well. This is easily done using pvc pipe and draped fabric. The fabric draping will change depending on your scenes.

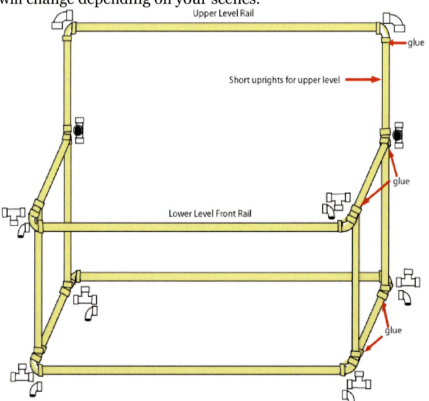

Practice your show and perform it for an audience.

☺ ☻ ☻ EXPLORATION: Be An Imagineer

Design your own amusement park ride. It could be simple ride like a new roller coaster, or a full attraction ride like the Imagineers at Disney design. At Disney they say, "If you can dream it, you can build it." Don't be inhibited by what's already out there. Make a list of ten things you wish you could

First North Americans – North America – Salts – Creative Kids

experience. Choose one of them and then design a ride that fulfills that wish!

☺ ☺ ☺ **EXPLORATION: Dance To The Music**
You'll need to start with a recording of a song you really like. When you're choosing your music, consider the genre, speed, and overall feel of the dance you'd like to create. Choreograph an original dance to the song. Consider your costume, lighting, and any background/stage/prop elements you may need. Practice the dance to perfection, then perform it for an audience.

☺ ☺ ☺ **EXPLORATION: Invention Convention**
Create your own new invention. What would make life easier or better?

Begin by making a sketch of your invention. Diagram and describe its parts and functions. Write a description of how it will work. If possible, build a model or prototype of the invention. Name your invention and prepare a marketing plan. How much will it cost to build? How much will you sell it for? Where could you purchase it? Present your invention to an audience and describe it; convince them they need one!

☺ ☺ ☺ **EXPLORATION: Third Time's A Charm**
Look through your art portfolio or sketchbook and choose a piece of artwork. Now make three different versions of it. For example, if you made a watercolor painting, you might make a 3-D version of it with scrap wood, screws, and paint. You might do a detailed chalk sidewalk drawing. You could make it into pillowcase or skirt. You could turn it into a mosaic, a pointillism drawing, or a collage. Whatever you choose, make 3 very different versions of the same piece.

☺ ☺ **EXPLORATION: Chef in Training**
Create a meal that suits your taste. You can look through recipe books for ideas if you'd like, but don't just re-create what they've done. Add or change some of the ingredients. You may want to think about the design of the dish along with the taste. Sometimes the look of the dish can be as exciting as the flavor. Name your dish and be prepared to describe it. You may want to prepare several side dishes to accompany your creation. Your dish may be more on the fun, creative side, or it could be more traditional, but whatever you make, make it a work of art.

Arrange a dinner to serve your new dish at. Set a beautiful table – consider dishes, place mats, place cards, and centerpieces. You could even plan a theme dinner.

Famous Folks

Louis Braille invented the Braille method of reading for blind people when he was just fifteen years old.

Famous Folks

Pablo Picasso completed his first painting *Le Picador* in 1889 at the age of nine.

His technique improved as he practiced and practiced. His style also changed as he got older. Look at some of his other art.

First North Americans – North America – Salts – Creative Kids

Famous Folks

In 1962, when he was six years old, Robert Patch submitted an invention for a patent which was granted. The invention? A toy truck.

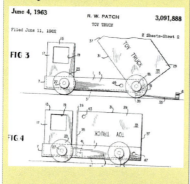

If your kids are like me then stories of child prodigies are just depressing. They leave you feeling not so much like . . .wow, I can do it too . . . as dang it, here I am completely talentless.

Part of the problem is I think that we don't recognize great talent when we see it because we're looking for art, or music, or a cool invention we can touch with our hands. We forget the talents of love and friendship, and listening and common sense. Not to mention that talent for mastering every Mario game invented. The other part of the problem is that to really develop a talent you have to spend as much time on it as you spent mastering Mario 3.

☺ ☺ ☺ **EXPLORATION: 10 Ingredient Free Art**

For this exploration, you can make anything you want! You are limited only by your supplies. Have someone choose ten art supplies for you. Using only those ten items, create an interesting, original art piece. Here's a list of supplies to consider:

- paper (lots of kinds to choose from)
- pencil
- markers
- colored pencils
- chalks
- crayons
- oil pastels
- glue (lots of kinds to choose from)
- tape
- paints (choose from tempera, watercolor, finger paints, oil paints, acrylics)
- paintbrushes
- pom poms
- foam shapes
- stickers
- pipe cleaners
- wiggly eyes
- glitter
- cotton balls
- wood
- clay
- paper plates and cups
- feathers
- yarn
- fabric
- wire
- milk cartons or other empty food packaging
- straws
- foil, plastic wrap, waxed paper
- balloons
- small household items (marbles, tiles, picture frames, dishes)
- natural items (leaves, shells, stones, bark, dirt)
- food items (beans, rice, sugar, pasta noodles, dry dog food, etc.)

- egg cartons
- cardboard
- tissue paper
- toilet paper rolls
- paper towel rolls
- nuts, bolts, screws, nails
- jewelry making supplies like beads, brackets, wire, and clips
- ribbon

☺ ☺ ☺ EXPLORATION: Movie Maker
Write your own movie script and create a short film. You can either act in it, or be the director and recruit help for the acting portion. Make sure you have a full script with stage directions and lines, costumes, make-up, a cameraman, sound effects, and music.

You will need to film it in segments most likely, and then put it together using editing software.

EXPLANATION: Exercising Imagination
Young children are creatively uninhibited. A 3 to 5 year old typically won't hesitate when it comes to artistic pursuits. They feel totally confident about dancing, singing, drawing, and exhibiting all kinds of creativity. By age 10 or so, they often experience a crisis of creativity. All of sudden they don't feel capable of doing anything original or creative. They have trouble coming up with ideas, would rather imitate someone else, and then often express that their work just isn't as good. This is partly a product of our imitation-style of learning. They're imaginations are out of shape!

☺ ☺ ☺ EXPLORATION: Photography 14-Day Challenge
Take 14 pictures over 14 days.
Day 1: A picture of something you love
Day 2: Your favorite book
Day 3: Eyes
Day 4: A picture taken from a very low vantage point
Day 5: A picture taken from a very high vantage point
Day 6: The sky
Day 7: Something that makes you laugh
Day 8: Night
Day 9: Still life scene you set up

Explanation
If your child really begins to develop an interest in a particular area then do your best to support them by buying the proper tools. Don't make your budding artist struggle through with cheapo plastic toy paint brushes. Supply your little chef with good knives and teach her to use them safely. And scare up real instruments, not toys, for your musician.

Teachers and classes can be super important too, wherever you can afford them. If you can't afford them then figure out how to trade for lessons or how your child can earn the money for their own lessons whenever possible.

Teaching Tip
Allow opportunities for creativity in other assignments as well. A simple way to do this is to NOT provide an perfectly made example of what you'd like them to do. Describe the assignment, but don't always give a visual for them to re-create.

First North Americans – North America – Salts – Creative Kids

Art Out of the Box

Don't be constrained by the traditional uses of art supplies. Household objects could be used as tools to apply paint with if a paintbrush isn't one of the provided supplies. What else can you use in new ways?

Go to a specific kind of store, like a pet store or hardware store, and search for interesting items that could be used to create art with.

Teaching Tip

Often we feel that we should only do things we excel at, but in truth, the way to improve is to fail over and over again.

Talk about failure, endurance, and creativity throughout this unit. How are they related?

Day 10: A group of people
Day 11: Water
Day 12: Two things that don't go together
Day 13: A silhouette
Day 14: Self portrait

☺ ☺ ☺ EXPLORATION: Set a Goal

If one of your projects struck a creative chord within you, set a goal to work more in that area. If drawing, dance, music, invention, photography, cooking, or another creative pursuit is fun for you, fuel that fun and it might just become a passion. Write down three things you can do to improve your skills in an area you have interest. For example, if you really enjoyed cooking during this unit, you could plan to cook dinner one night a week for the next month, invent a new dessert recipe, and begin compiling your very own recipe book. Whatever your interest, find ways to feed it and help your talent grow.

EXPLANATION: Mentors

Many talents can be pursued individually, but often it helps when we have a mentor. A child's role is to set goals and pursue things they are interested in. A parent's role is either to be a mentor or find a mentor for their child.

If Johnny is excited about photography, but it's not your forte, find him someone to partner with who shares his passion. This could be another kid who's learning, but ideally, it would be someone who has already developed their talent in photography and would be willing to take Johnny under his wing and show him how to really grow his photography skills.

Coming up next . . .

Unit 1-16

Ancient South America
South America – Plants
South American Art

First North Americans – North America – Salts – Creative Kids

My Ideas For This Unit:

Title: _____ Topic: _____

_____
_____
_____
_____
_____
_____
_____
_____
_____
_____

Title: _____ Topic: _____

_____
_____
_____
_____
_____
_____
_____
_____
_____
_____

Title: _____ Topic: _____

_____
_____
_____
_____
_____
_____
_____
_____
_____
_____

First North Americans – North America – Salts – Creative Kids

My Ideas For This Unit:

Title: _____   Topic: _____

_____
_____
_____
_____
_____
_____
_____
_____
_____

Title: _____   Topic: _____

_____
_____
_____
_____
_____
_____
_____
_____
_____
_____

Title: _____   Topic: _____

_____
_____
_____
_____
_____
_____
_____
_____
_____

Ancient North American Homes

These are buildings from North American cultures of the Ohio Valley. The walls are built of posts and covered with mud, similar to wattle and daub houses of ancient Europe. The roofs are thatch. The little building is on stilts to keep it out of the water and away from critters. It is where the people who live in the house store their harvest of maize and other crops.

Ancient North America: Unit I-15

1200-400BC	1000-300BC	300BC-550AD	300BC-900AD
 Olmec people	 Adena people	 Hopewell people	 Maya people

5000 BC	32 BC	1000 AD
 Corn (maize) is systematically bred to resemble modern forms.	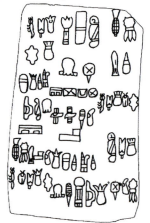 Olmecs begin to use zero as a place holder in calculations	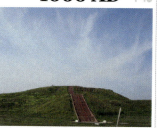 City of Chahokia (near St. Louis) rises

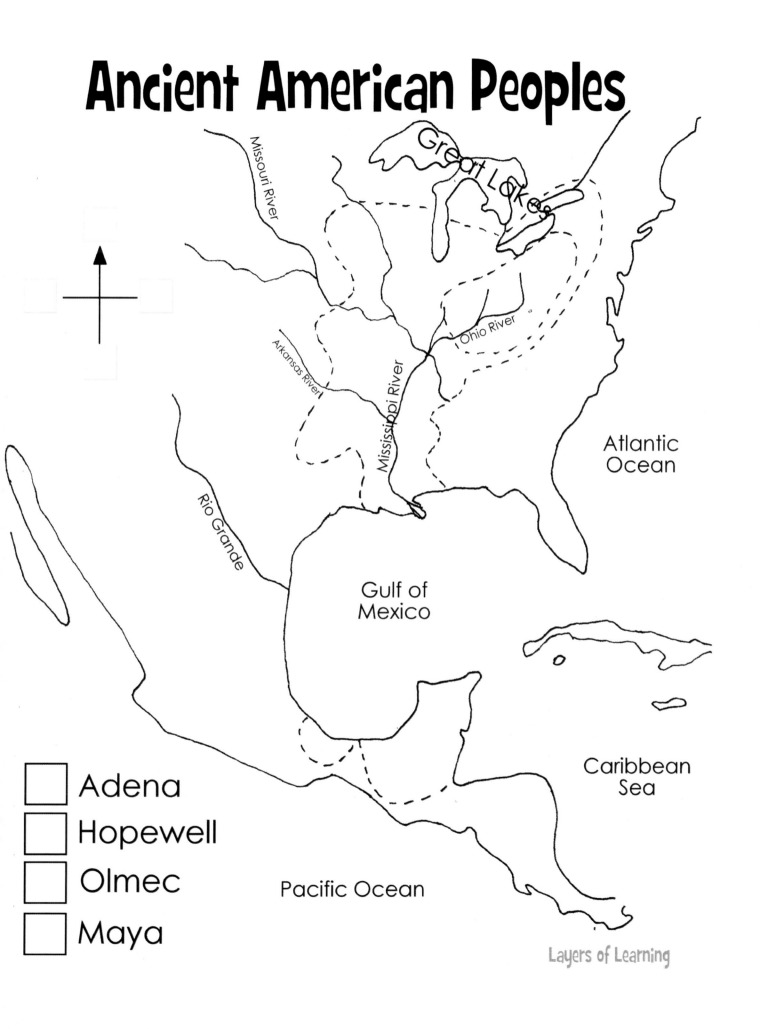

Who Built the Wisconsin Mounds?

Who built the mounds of Wisconsin? From the advent of the whites the problem of the mound builders has been a more intricate one than it was when the scientific world was wrestling with the curious earth structures in Ohio and other older sections of the country. There is a strange individuality in the earth-works of Wisconsin, different from those of other parts, and the most perplexing thing about the problem is whether the builders here were the originators of the work, or did they attempt to copy the structures of other aboriginal peoples? The Indians found here by the first whites were ignorant of the origin or purpose of the mounds, although we read occasionally of their using the circular heaps of earth in some of their ceremonials. But they claimed to know nothing of their building nor of their builders.

The most common forms in which these mounds were constructed and in which the whites found them are, round mole hills, called tumulus; in imitation of birds and animals, called effigy mounds, and long horizontal ridges. Probably the tumuli are the most numerous, and these are in all sizes. One of the largest in this vicinity is about four miles southwest of Prairie du Sac, when measures 63 feet in diameter across the base and is now 13 feet in height at the summit. This stands in the woods and has not been leveled in an attempt to work the land. Many are not more than two or three feet in height, and a large percentage of those that were found by early settlers are entirely obliterated by years of plowing and harrowing. Of the effigy mounds those in the form of birds are most numerous, although there are plenty that mark the outlines of the lizard, deer, bear and other animals so plainly that nobody can mistake the intent of the artists who shaped them. Some of the bird mounds are especially attractive to look upon. Many are very large, the one shown here having a stretch of wing clearly marked of 396 feet.

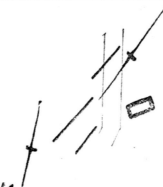

A Symmetrical Bird Mound.

quarter of a mile in length. The quarter part of these are of the tumulus variety, although there are many effigies and parallelograms. This group is on the west side of the Wisconsin river near Kilbourn. The old stage road between Kilbourn and Baraboo cuts through this group, a fragment of which is shown below:

The body has a width of 14 feet and the elevation above the surrounding soil is two and a half feet. As one stands upon the body the whole outline is so perfect that he cannot mistake it. Many of them are much smaller. One of the most perfect specimens near Madison is on the shores of Devil's lake at Kirkland. Although in front of the old hotel where thousands have tramped over it for years, the lines are yet perfect. It has a stretch of about 110 feet from tip to tip.

There is up in Sauk county, four miles northeast of Baraboo, a man mound that has attracted visitors from all over this country and Europe. Of the few man mounds known, this is the most perfect. It has an extreme length of 290 feet, with arms, legs and feet perfectly outlined and is capped with a headdress that has the general look of feathers. This is on land not cultivated, and is in a good state of preservation, except that the legs have been cut in two by the public road.

Man Mound.

In many places they are in groups, as large a number as 63 having been located in a row not more than a good state of preservation. About the only point on which scientists are agreed relative to these mounds is that they prove that this section was once densely populated. No such Indian settlements as we have knowledge of could have built them. In about every instance the earth from which they were constructed was carried—it is different from the soil on which the mounds rest. The earth from which a large tumulus was made came at least 40 rods; there is no soil like that in the mound nearer than that. Of course these earthworks were much larger when built, and their present size is no mark of the labor required to build them. Centuries of freezing and thawing, rain and sunshine have reduced them more than half. With the crude appliances of the aborigines for digging and carrying the earth, it must have required an army of people a long time to build them. The question remains unsolved, who built the Wisconsin mounds?

An Interesting Group.

Here is shown two bird mounds, three ridges, a tumulus and what was, probably the wall for a dwelling. All are greatly reduced, the upper bird mound being nearly 400 feet in length. There are many mounds about lakes Mendota and Monona, but no systematic effort has been made to survey, plat and preserve them. Two or three are on the university grounds and on the hills beyond are many more. In Sauk county the historical society has been making a thorough survey of the aboriginal earthworks in that section and has covered seven townships of the county. In these were located 734 mounds, one-half of which are in a

Photograph by Thelmadatter and shared on Wikimedia commons.

Layers of Learning

North America

North America

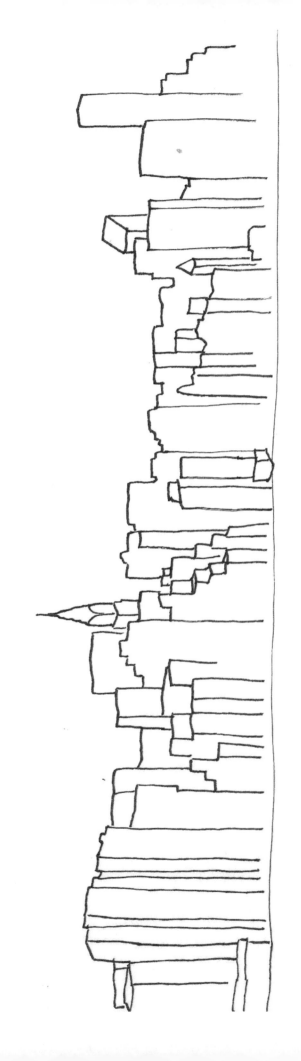

Mexico

- Desert
- Forest
- Pasture land
- Farmland

Periodic Table of the Elements

1 H Hydrogen 1.0																	2 He Helium 4.0
3 Li Lithium 6.9	4 Be Beryllium 9.0											5 B Boron 10.8	6 C Carbon 12.0	7 N Nitrogen 14.0	8 O Oxygen 16.0	9 F Fluorine 19.0	10 Ne Neon 20.2
11 Na Sodium 23.0	12 Mg Magnesium 24.3											13 Al Aluminum 27.0	14 Si Silicon 28.1	15 P Phosphorus 31.0	16 S Sulfur 32.1	17 Cl Chlorine 35.5	18 Ar Argon 40.0
19 K Potassium 39.1	20 Ca Calcium 40.1	21 Sc Scandium 45.0	22 Ti Titanium 47.9	23 V Vanadium 50.9	24 Cr Chromium 52.0	25 Mn Manganese 54.9	26 Fe Iron 55.9	27 Co Cobalt 58.9	28 Ni Nickel 58.7	29 Cu Copper 63.5	30 Zn Zinc 65.4	31 Ga Gallium 69.7	32 Ge Germanium 72.6	33 As Arsenic 74.9	34 Se Selenium 79.0	35 Br Bromine 79.9	36 Kr Krypton 83.8
37 Rb Rubidium 85.5	38 Sr Strontium 87.6	39 Y Yttrium 88.9	40 Zr Zirconium 91.2	41 Nb Niobium 92.9	42 Mo Molybdenum 95.9	43 Tc Technetium 99	44 Ru Ruthenium 101.0	45 Rh Rhodium 102.9	46 Pd Palladium 106.4	47 Ag Silver 107.9	48 Cd Cadmium 112.4	49 In Indium 114.8	50 Sn Tin 118.7	51 Sb Antimony 121.8	52 Te Tellurium 127.6	53 I Iodine 126.9	54 Xe Xenon 131.3
55 Cs Cesium 132.9	56 Ba Barium 137.3	Lanthinides 57-71	72 Hf Hafnium 178.5	73 Ta Tantalum 180.9	74 W Tungsten 183.9	75 Re Rhenium 186.2	76 Os Osmium 190.2	77 Ir Iridium 192.2	78 Pt Platinum 195.1	79 Au Gold 197.0	80 Hg Mercury 200.6	81 Tl Thallium 204.4	82 Pb Lead 207.2	83 Bi Bismuth 209.0	84 Po Polonium 210.0	85 At Astatine 211	86 Rn Radon 222.0
87 Fr Francium 223.0	88 Ra Radium 226.0	Actinides 89-103	104 Rf Rutherfordium 267	105 Db Dubnium 268	106 Sg Seaborgium 271	107 Bh Bohrium 272	108 Hs Hassium 270	109 Mt Meitnerium 276	110 Ds Darmstadium 281	111 Rg Roentgenium 280	112 Cn Copernicium 285	113 Uut Ununtrium 284	114 Fl Flerovium 289	115 Uup Ununpentium 288	116 Lv Livermorium 293	117 Uus Ununseptium 294	118 Uuo Ununoctium 294

57 La Lanthanum 138.9	58 Ce Cerium 140.1	59 Pr Praseodymium 140.9	60 Nd Neodymium 144.2	61 Pm Promethium 145	62 Sm Samarium 150.4	63 Eu Europium 152.0	64 Gd Gadolinium 157.3	65 Tb Terbium 158.9	66 Dy Dysprosium 162.5	67 Ho Holmium 164.0	68 Er Erbium 167.3	69 Tm Thulium 168.9	70 Yb Ytterbium 173.0	71 Lu Lutetium 175.0
89 Ac Actinium 227.0	90 Th Thorium 232.0	91 Pa Protactinium 231.0	92 U Uranium 238.0	93 Np Neptunium 237	94 Pu Plutonium 242	95 Am Americium 243	96 Cm Curium 247	97 Bk Berkelium 247	98 Cf Californium 251	99 Es Einsteinium 254	100 Fm Fermium 253	101 Md Mendelevium 256	102 No Nobelium 254	103 Lr Lawrencium 257

Layers of Learning

Half-Life Equations

A half-life is the amount of time it takes for half of a sample of a radioactive element to decay.

> Radon-222 has a half-life of 3.8 days. If you start with a 100g sample, how much is left after 15.2 days?
>
> 15.2 days × (1 half-life) / (3.8 days) = 4 half-lives
>
> 1 half-life = 50g
> 2 half-lives = 25g
> 3 half-lives = 12.5g
> 4 half-lives = **6.25g**

1. Carbon-14 has a half-life of 5730 years. If you start with a 100g sample, how much will be left after 11,460 years?

2. If 100g of gold-198 has a half-life of 2.696 days, how much will you have left after 8.088 days?

3. Radon-226 has a half-life of 1600 years. How long will it take for a 28g sample of Radon to decay to 3.5g?

Half-Life Equations

A half-life is the amount of time it takes for half of a sample of a radioactive element to decay.

Radon-222 has a half-life of 3.8 days. If you start with a 100g sample, how much is left after 15.2 days?

$$15.2 \text{ days} \times \frac{1 \text{ half-life}}{3.8 \text{ days}} = 4 \text{ half-lives}$$

1 half-life = 50g
2 half-lives = 25g
3 half-lives = 12.5g
4 half-lives = **6.25g**

---

1. Carbon-14 has a half-life of 5730 years. If you start with a 100g sample, how much will be left after 11,460 years?

$$11460 \times \frac{1 \text{ half-life}}{5730} = 2 \text{ half-lives}$$

1 half life = 50
2 half-lives = **25**

2. If 1g of gold-198 has a half-life of 2.696 days, how much will you have left after 8.088 days?

$$8.088 \times \frac{1 \text{ half-life}}{2.696} = 3$$

1 half-life = .5
2 half lives = .25
3 half lives = **.125**

3. Radon-226 has a half-life of 1600 years. How long will it take for a 28g sample of Radon to decay to 3.5g?

3 half lives = 3.5 x 2 = 7 x 2 = 14 x 2 = 28

3 x 1600 = **4800 years**

ABOUT THE AUTHORS

Karen & Michelle . . .
Mothers, sisters, teachers, women who are passionate
about educating kids.
We are dedicated to lifelong learning.

Karen, a mother of four, who has homeschooled her kids for more than eight years with her husband, Bob, has a bachelor's degree in child development with an emphasis in education. She lives in Utah where she gardens, teaches piano, and plays an excruciating number of board games with her kids. Karen is our resident Arts expert and English guru {most necessary as Michelle regularly and carelessly mangles the English language and occasionally steps over the bounds of polite society}.

Michelle and her husband, Cameron, homeschooling now for over a decade, teach their six boys on their ten acres in beautiful Idaho country. Michelle earned a bachelor's in biology, making her the resident Science expert, though she is mocked by her friends for being the *Botanist with the Black Thumb of Death*. She also is the go-to for History and Government. She believes in staying up late, hot chocolate, and a no whining policy. We both pitch in on Geography, in case you were wondering, and are on a continual quest for knowledge.

*Visit our constantly updated blog for tons of free ideas,
free printables, and more cool stuff for sale:*
www.Layers-of-Learning.com

Made in the USA
Middletown, DE
29 December 2019